Notes to the Future

ATRIA BOOKS

NEW YORK LONDON TORONTO SYDNEY NEW DELHI

NOTES TO THE FUTURE

WORDS OF WISDOM

NELSON MANDELA

Introduction by Archbishop Desmond Tutu
Editors: Sello Hatang and Sahm Venter
Associate Editor: Doug Abrams

ATRIA BOOKS
A Division of Simon & Schuster, Inc.
1230 Avenue of the Americas
New York, NY 10020

First Atria Books hardcover edition November 2012 in association with PQ Blackwell

ATRIA BOOKS and colophon are trademarks of Simon & Schuster, Inc.

First produced and originated by PQ Blackwell Limited, 116 Symonds Street, Auckland 1010, New Zealand (www.pqblackwell.com)

For information about special discounts for bulk purchases, please contact Simon & Schuster Special Sales at 1-866-506-1949 or business@simonandschuster.com.

The Simon & Schuster Speakers Bureau can bring authors to your live event. For more information or to book an event contact the Simon & Schuster Speakers Bureau at 1-866-248-3049 or visit our website at www.simonspeakers.com.

Designed by Ruth Lee-Mui

Manufactured in the United States of America

10 9 8 7 6 5 4 3 2 1

Library of Congress Cataloging-in-Publication Data is available.

ISBN 978–1–4516–7539–9
ISBN 978–1–4516–7541–2 (ebook)

A good pen can also remind us of the happiest moments in our lives, bring noble ideas into our dens, our blood and our souls. It can turn tragedy into hope and victory.

From a letter to Zindzi Mandela,
written on Robben Island, February 10, 1980

CONTENTS

Introduction by Archbishop Desmond Tutu xi

PART ONE: STRUGGLE

On Whose Shoulders We Stand 2
If I Had My Time Over 4
What I Stood For 6
Enemies of Racism 8
Cease Thinking in Terms of Color 10
I Had Come of Age as a Freedom Fighter 12
I Planned Sabotage 14
If I Must Die 16
Courage Was Not the Absence of Fear 18
I Could Not Give Myself Up to Despair 20
When We Decided to Take Up Arms 22
The Most Powerful Weapon Is Not Violence 24
Freedom Can Never Be Taken for Granted 26

For the Love of Freedom 28
The Arrest Itself 30
Prison Not Only Robs You of Your Freedom 32
They Wanted to Break Our Spirits 34
Prison Was a Kind of Crucible 36
Writing a Letter in Prison 38
The False Image 40
A Virtually Widowed Woman 42
The Oppressed and the Oppressor Alike 44
The Noble Chorus 46

PART TWO: VICTORY

I Greet You All in the Name of Peace 50
The First Democratically Elected President 52
The Freedoms Which Democracy Brings 54
Compromise Is the Only Alternative 56
If You Are Negotiating 58
To Cast My First Vote 60
A Real Leader 62
We Chose Reconciliation 64
We Have to Forgive the Past 66
I Am Not Particularly Religious 68
We Need Religious Institutions 70
Our Differences Are Our Strength 72

PART THREE: WISDOM

None of Us Is a Superstar 76
Peace Is the Greatest Weapon 78

Character of Growth 80
Masters of Our Own Fate 82
Turn Our Common Suffering into Hope 84
Who Are Full of Contradictions 86
The Capacity of Memory 88
Tested and Dependable Friends 90
Rising Every Time You Fall 92
I Have Stumbled 94
For Humanity to Produce Saints 96
No Power on Earth That Can Compare 98
Education Is the Great Engine 100
My Favorite Pastime 102
I Speak of Culture 104
Ahead of the Children 106
Just Because of Your Grey Hair 108
It Must Not Disturb My Hair 110
Sport Has the Power to Change the World 112
Being a Hero 114
A Streak of Goodness 116
What Difference We Have Made 118
No One Is Born Hating Another Person 120
Preparing a Master Plan 122
We Have Learned the Lesson 124
The Time Has Come for Me to Take Leave 126

PART FOUR: FUTURE

It Was My Duty 130
The Future Belongs to Our Youth 132

The Only Basis of Human Happiness 134
AIDS Is No Longer Just a Disease 136
The Eradication of Poverty 138
Trapped in the Prison of Poverty 140
The Role and Place of Women 142
Criticism Is Necessary for Any Society 144
A Culture of Caring 146
The Foundation of One's Spiritual Life 148
Human Rights Are Ingrained 150
No Country However Powerful 152
The Keeper of Our Brother and Sister 154
All Parts of Our Planet 156
Defy Today's Merchants of Cynicism 158
The Only Road Open 160
A Bright Future Beckons 162

Nobel Peace Prize Acceptance Speech, 1993 165
Acknowledgments 173
Bibliography 175

INTRODUCTION

Archbishop Desmond Tutu

The book that you hold in your hand is nothing short of a miracle. The words it contains were denied to the world for almost four decades. From December of 1952 when Nelson Rolihlahla Mandela was banned by the apartheid government until his glorious release in February 1990, it was a crime punishable by imprisonment to quote him or his writings. Mandela had been all but silenced. His words were only spoken, if they were spoken at all, in hushed whispers of defiance or smuggled out of prison and released by those in exile. The fact that Mandela is now one of the most quoted people in the world is an extraordinary turnaround and a testament to the fact that the truth cannot be silenced and wisdom cannot be stopped.

• • •

The words in this book are those of the most admired and revered political leader in the world and one of the greatest human beings to walk this earth. Why does he turn people's knees to water? Not because he has power in any conventional sense. He was not commander-in-chief of a large military power. But what the world recognizes is his moral power. When the world is asked who are the great people, they usually don't mention great generals. In our best moments and deep inside us, we know that goodness and righteousness and courage are admirable attributes that we crave. Isn't it fascinating that we may envy and even respect the driven, successful businessperson, but we are seldom moved to love them? Yet what happens when the world is confronted by a Gandhi, a Mother Teresa, or a Mandela? We thrill, we admire them, we even get to adore and love them. We recognize their goodness and want to emulate it. We want to quote their words and live by them.

Gathered here are Mandela's most inspiring and most enduring quotes that will live on for generations. They are not the ephemeral words of the politician, but the eternal words of the statesperson. They are not the timely words of the activist, but the timeless words of the humanitarian. And throughout, you will see the great humanity, humor, and hope that allowed him to endure twenty-seven years in prison and come out ennobled by the experience. You will see the man who used every moment of his imprisonment to improve himself and his comrades so they would be ready for rule. You will see the man who was greater than the legends that had formed during his long absence: forgiving to his jailors, gracious to his former enemies, seeking reconciliation for his country, and letting go of power humbly in the end.

Many of these quotes are published here for the first time, and come from his prison letters to his wife, children, and friends as well as his unpublished autobiographical manuscript written on Robben Island. In these pages, you also will find his most famous and cherished words.

Even in this day and age, when so many quotes—and often misquotes—are available online, there is nothing quite like sitting down and reading through these quotations end to end. It is like a visit with our most eminent global elder, who generously offers his wisdom for all to learn. It is like sitting down for a cup of rooibos tea and having an extended conversation with this great man.

In prison, Mandela learned the power of words, and it was only through his poignant notes, cherished letters, or smuggled statements that he was able to free his mind from its imprisonment. But there is another prison, one that none of us escapes. It is a prison not in space but in time. It is our mortality. This collection, of his most memorable and enduring quotes, is presented in the hope that it may free his words from this prison and allow future generations to hear his once banned words, to take inspiration from his courageous example, and to seek freedom and justice and democracy for all. These are Mandela's notes to the future. Read them, reread them, and live by them. History calls each of us in our own way and in our own time. We are all capable of greatness, and the world needs yours.

Cape Town, South Africa, June 2011

It is never my custom to use words lightly. If twenty-seven years in prison have done anything to us, it was to use the silence of solitude to make us understand how precious words are and how real speech is in its impact on the way people live and die.

Closing address at the XIII International AIDS Conference, Durban, South Africa, July 14, 2000

Part One

STRUGGLE

You can see that "there is no easy walk to freedom anywhere" and many of us will have to pass through the valley of the shadow of death again and again before we reach the mountain tops of our desires.

Quoting Jawaharlal Nehru, from a presidential address to the ANC Transvaal Congress, also known as the "No Easy Walk to Freedom" speech, Transvaal, South Africa, September 21, 1953

On Whose Shoulders We Stand

We should never forget those on whose shoulders we stand and those who paid the supreme price for freedom.

Upon receiving the Freedom of Howick,
Howick, South Africa, December 12, 1996

To the extent that I have been able to achieve anything, I know that this is because I am the product of the people of South Africa.

Final sitting of the first democratically elected Parliament,
Cape Town, South Africa, March 26, 1999

We come from a people who, because they would not accept to be treated as subhuman, redeemed the dignity of all humanity everywhere.

From an address to the Parliament of Canada,
Ottawa, Canada, June 18, 1990

If I Had My Time Over

I have often wondered whether a person is justified in neglecting his own family to fight for opportunities for others.

From an unpublished autobiographical manuscript,
written on Robben Island, 1975

If I had my time over I would do the same again. So would any man who dares call himself a man.

From an address to the court on charges of
inciting workers to strike and leaving the country illegally,
Old Synagogue, Pretoria, South Africa, November 7, 1962

There are many things that disturb you when children grow without you.

From the documentary *Mandela: The Living Legend,* 2003

One of the dreams I constantly had in prison was me going home and getting out in the middle of the city and having to walk from town to Soweto and reaching home, finding that the house was open, that there was nobody at home and being concerned as to what had happened to Winnie and the children.

From a BBC (UK) documentary, 1996

I myself did not realize the full implications of the life I had chosen.

From an interview, circa 1993

What I Stood For

I was made, by the law, a criminal, not because of what I had done, but because of what I stood for, because of what I thought, because of my conscience.

From an address to the court on charges of
inciting workers to strike and leaving the country illegally,
Old Synagogue, Pretoria, South Africa, November 7, 1962

I can only say that I felt morally obliged to do what I did.

Speech from the dock, Rivonia Trial, Palace of Justice,
Pretoria, South Africa, April 20, 1964

It would have been immoral to keep quiet while a racist tyranny sought to reduce an entire people into a status worse than that of the beasts of the forest.

From an address to a joint session of the Houses of Congress, Washington DC, USA, June 26, 1990

It will forever remain an accusation and a challenge to all men and women of conscience that it took as long as it has, before all of us stood up to say enough is enough.

From an address to the United Nations Special Committee against Apartheid, United Nations, New York, USA, June 22, 1990

Enemies of Racism

I want at once to make it clear that I am no racialist, and I detest racialism, because I regard it as a barbaric thing, whether it comes from a black man or from a white man.

From an application for the recusal of the Magistrate
Mr. W. A. Van Helsdingen, Old Synagogue,
Pretoria, South Africa, October 22, 1962

We of the ANC had always stood for a non-racial democracy, and we shrank from any action which might drive the races further apart than they already were. But the hard facts were that fifty years of non-violence had brought the African people nothing but more and more repressive legislation, and fewer and fewer rights.

Speech from the dock, Rivonia Trial, Palace of Justice,
Pretoria, South Africa, April 20, 1964

I detest white supremacy and will fight it with every weapon in my hands.

From a letter to General Du Preez, Commissioner of Prisons, written on Robben Island, July 12, 1976

Science and experience have also shown that no race is inherently superior to others, and this myth has been equally exploded whenever blacks and whites are given equal opportunity for development.

From an essay titled "Whither the Black Consciousness Movement," written on Robben Island, 1978

What we are is enemies of racism and oppression.

ANC National Conference on reconstruction and strategy, South Africa, January 21, 1994

CEASE THINKING IN TERMS OF COLOR

We are extricating ourselves from a system that insulted our common humanity by dividing us from one another on the basis of race and setting us against each other [as] oppressed and oppressor.

Upon receiving the report of the TRC (Truth and Reconciliation Commission), Pretoria, South Africa, October 29, 1998

We slaughter one another in our words and attitudes. We slaughter one another in the stereotypes and mistrust that linger in our heads, and the words of hate we spew from our lips.

State of the Nation address, Parliament, Cape Town, South Africa, February 5, 1999

We are fighting for a society where people will cease thinking in terms of color.

From a conversation with Richard Stengel, March 8, 1993

If there is one lesson we can learn from the struggle against racism, in our country as well as yours, it is that racism must be consciously combatted, and not discreetly tolerated.

Investiture, Clark University, Atlanta, Georgia, USA, July 10, 1993

I HAD COME OF AGE AS A FREEDOM FIGHTER

To overthrow oppression has been sanctioned by humanity and is the highest aspiration of every free man.

From a presidential address to the ANC Transvaal Congress,
also known as the "No Easy Walk to Freedom" speech,
Transvaal, South Africa, September 21, 1953

A new world will be won not by those who stand at a distance with their arms folded, but by those who are in the arena, whose garments are torn by storms and whose bodies are maimed in the course of the contest.

From a letter to Winnie Mandela,
written on Robben Island, June 23, 1969

The campaign freed me from any lingering sense of doubt or inferiority I might still have felt; it liberated me from the feeling of being overwhelmed by the power and seeming invincibility of the white man and his institutions. But now the white man had felt the power of my punches and I could walk upright like a man, and look everyone in the eye with the dignity that comes from not having succumbed to oppression and fear. I had come of age as a freedom fighter.

From *Long Walk to Freedom,* 1994

Banning not only confines one physically, it imprisons one's spirit. It induces a kind of psychological claustrophobia that makes one yearn for not only freedom of movement but spiritual escape.

From *Long Walk to Freedom,* 1994

I Planned Sabotage

All lawful modes of expressing opposition to this principle had been closed by legislation, and we were placed in a position in which we had either to accept a permanent state of inferiority, or to defy the government. We chose to defy the law.

Speech from the dock, Rivonia Trial, Palace of Justice,
Pretoria, South Africa, April 20, 1964

I consider myself neither legally nor morally bound to obey laws made by a Parliament in which I have no representation.

From an application for the recusal of the Magistrate
Mr. W. A. Van Helsdingen, Old Synagogue,
Pretoria, South Africa, October 22, 1962

I do not, however, deny that I planned sabotage. I did not plan it in a spirit of recklessness, nor because I have any love of violence. I planned it as a result of a calm and sober assessment of the political situation that had arisen after many years of tyranny, exploitation and oppression of my people by the whites.

Speech from the dock, Rivonia Trial, Palace of Justice,
Pretoria, South Africa, April 20, 1964

When a man is denied the right to live the life he believes in, he has no choice but to become an outlaw.

Source unknown, 1994

If I Must Die

If I must die, let me declare for all to know that I will meet my fate like a man.

From a note written hours before his sentencing in the Rivonia Trial, Pretoria, South Africa, June 12, 1964

I was prepared for the death penalty. To be truly prepared for something, one must actually expect it. One cannot be prepared for something while secretly believing it will not happen. We were all prepared, not because we were brave but because we were realistic.

From *Long Walk to Freedom*, 1994

Death is a frightful disaster no matter what the cause and the age of the person affected.

From a letter to Irene Buthelezi, on receiving the news of his son Thembi's death, written on Robben Island, August 3,1969

Death is something inevitable. When a man has done what he considers to be his duty to his people and his country, he can rest in peace. I believe I have made that effort and that is, therefore, why I will sleep for the eternity.

From the documentary *Mandela,* 1996

Courage Was Not the Absence of Fear

Since the dawn of history, mankind has honored and respected brave and honest people.

From a letter to Winnie Mandela,
written on Robben Island, June 23, 1969

I learned that courage was not the absence of fear, but the triumph over it. I felt fear myself more times than I can remember, but I hid it behind a mask of boldness. The brave man is not he who does not feel afraid, but he who conquers that fear.

From *Long Walk to Freedom*, 1994

I can pretend that I am brave, you know, and [that] I can beat the whole world.

From a conversation with Richard Stengel, March 18, 1993

I was with brave colleagues; they appeared to be braver than myself. I would like to put that on record.

From a conversation with Ahmed Kathrada, circa 1993/94

I Could Not Give Myself Up to Despair

The realist, however shocked and disappointed by the frailties of those he adores, will look at human behavior from all sides objectively and will concentrate on those qualities in a person which are edifying, which lift your spirit [and] kindle one's enthusiasm to live.

From a letter to Winnie Mandela,
written on Robben Island, December 9, 1979

I am fundamentally an optimist. Whether that comes from nature or nurture, I cannot say. Part of being optimistic is keeping one's head pointed towards the sun, one's feet moving forward.

From *Long Walk to Freedom*, 1994

There were many dark moments when my faith in humanity was sorely tested, but I would not and could not give myself up to despair. That way lay defeat and death.

From *Long Walk to Freedom,* 1994

WHEN WE DECIDED TO TAKE UP ARMS

It was only when all else had failed, when all channels of peaceful protest had been barred to us, that the decision was made to embark on violent forms of political struggle.

Speech from the dock, Rivonia Trial, Palace of Justice, Pretoria, South Africa, April 20, 1964

When we decided to take up arms, it was because the only other choice was to surrender and to submit to slavery.

Forty-eighth National Conference of the ANC, Durban, South Africa, July 2, 1991

If we had peaceful channels of communication, we would never have thought of resorting to violence.

At home, Soweto, South Africa, February 1990

Although we had no hope of defeating the enemy in the battlefield, nevertheless, we fought back to keep the idea of liberation alive.

From a conversation with Richard Stengel, January 13, 1993

Through the years oppressed people have fought for their birthright by peaceful means, where that was possible, and through force where peaceful channels were closed.

From a memorandum to President P. W. Botha,
written in Victor Verster Prison, Paarl, South Africa, July 1989

The Most Powerful Weapon Is Not Violence

The most powerful weapon is not violence but it is talking to people.

From a BBC (UK) interview, October 28, 1993

For me, non-violence was not a moral principle but a strategy; there is no moral goodness in using an ineffective weapon.

From *Long Walk to Freedom,* 1994

Continuously, we have to fight to defeat the primitive tendency towards the glorification of arms, the adulation of force, born of the illusion that injustice can be perpetuated by the capacity to kill, or that disputes are necessarily best resolved by resort to violent means.

From an address to the fifty-third United Nations General Assembly, New York City, USA, September 21, 1998

In a world riven by violence and strife, Gandhi's message of peace and non-violence holds the key to human survival in the twenty-first century. He rightly believed in the efficacy of pitting the soul force of the Satyagraha against the brute force of the oppressor and, in effect, converting the oppressor to the right and moral point of view.

From a video message to the Satyagraha Centenary Conference, New Delhi, India, January 29–30, 2007

Freedom Can Never Be Taken for Granted

The purpose of freedom is to create it for others.

Prison desk calendar, written on Robben Island, June 2, 1979

Freedom is not only the absence of being in jail, just as it is always said that peace is not merely the absence of war.

From a Nobel Laureates interview with Lorie Karnath, April 2004

Real leaders must be ready to sacrifice all for the freedom of their people.

At the Chief Albert Luthuli Centenary Celebrations,
KwaDukuza, South Africa, April 25, 1998

Nothing can stop the evolution of humanity towards the condition of greater and ever-expanding freedom. While the voice of an individual can be condemned to silence by death, imprisonment and confinement, the spirit that drives people to seek liberty can never be stilled.

From a statement to the Parliament of the Republic of Ireland,
Dublin, Ireland, 2 July 2, 1990

Freedom can never be taken for granted. Each generation must safeguard it and extend it. Your parents and elders sacrificed much so that you should have freedom without suffering what they did. Use this precious right to ensure that the darkness of the past never returns.

From an address at the opening of the President's budget debate,
Parliament, Cape Town, South Africa, March 2, 1999

For the Love of Freedom

We do not want freedom without bread, nor do we want bread without freedom.

Investiture, Clark University, Atlanta, Georgia, USA, July 10, 1993

Too many have died since I went to prison. Too many have suffered for the love of freedom.

From a response to an offer of conditional freedom, read by Zindzi Mandela at a rally, Jabulani Stadium, Soweto, South Africa, February 10, 1985

I cherish my own freedom dearly, but I care even more for your freedom.

From a response to an offer of conditional freedom, read by Zindzi Mandela at a rally, Jabulani Stadium, Soweto, South Africa, February 10, 1985

The Arrest Itself

The arrest itself was done very courteously, very politely.

Revisiting the site of his August 5, 1962, arrest,
Howick, South Africa, November 15, 1993

The world around me literally crumbled, income disappeared and many obligations could not be honored.

From a letter to Zindzi Mandela, about being arrested for treason in 1956, written on Robben Island, March 1, 1981

Prison Not Only Robs You of Your Freedom

We were subject to harsh, if not brutal, treatment, and permanent physical and spiritual harm was caused to many prisoners.

From a letter to President P. W. Botha, written in Pollsmoor Prison, Cape Town, South Africa, February 13, 1985

Prison not only robs you of your freedom, it attempts to take away your identity.

From *Long Walk to Freedom,* 1994

To be alone in prison is a difficulty. You must never try it.

From a conversation with Richard Stengel, April 6, 1993

To go to prison because of your convictions, and be prepared to suffer for what you believe in, is something worthwhile. It is an achievement for a man to do his duty on earth irrespective of the consequences.

From an interview with Scott Macleod of *Time* magazine,
Soweto, South Africa, February 26, 1990

Sometimes I feel like one who is on the sidelines, who has missed life itself.

From a letter to Winnie Mandela,
written on Robben Island, January 21, 1979

They Wanted to Break Our Spirits

Prison and the authorities conspire to rob each man of his dignity. In and of itself, that assured that I would survive, for any man or institution that tries to rob me of my dignity will lose because I will not part with it at any price or under any pressure.

From *Long Walk to Freedom,* 1994

I have never regarded any man as my superior, either in my life outside or inside prison.

From a letter to General Du Preez, Commissioner of Prisons, written on Robben Island, July 12, 1976

I can't remember losing my sense of control; after all, in that situation you can only survive if you keep calm and cool.

At home, Soweto, South Africa, February 14, 1990

He had caused me to violate my self-control and I considered that a defeat at the hands of my opponent.

From *Long Walk to Freedom,* talking about a prison warder, 1994

They wanted to break our spirits. So what we did was to sing freedom songs as we were working and everybody was inspired.

From a conversation with Richard Stengel, December 8, 1992

There were some fellows, you know, who were good singers. I was not one of them, but I enjoyed singing.

From a conversation with Richard Stengel, December 14, 1992

I believe the way in which you will be treated by the prison authorities depends on your demeanor and you must fight that battle and win it on the very first day.

From a BBC (UK) documentary, 1996

PRISON WAS A KIND OF CRUCIBLE

It is only my flesh and bones that are shut up behind these tight walls. Otherwise I remain cosmopolitan in my outlook; in my thoughts I am as free as a falcon.

From a letter to Senator Douglas Lukhele,
written on Robben Island, August 1, 1970

Prison was a kind of crucible that tested a man's character. Some men, under the pressure of incarceration, showed true mettle, while others revealed themselves as less than what they had appeared to be.

From *Long Walk to Freedom,* 1994

Human beings have got the ability to adjust to anything.

From the documentary *Legends: Nelson Mandela,* 2005

Prison is itself a tremendous education in the need for patience and perseverance. It is, above all, a test of one's commitment. Those who passed through that school have all acquired a firmness, tempered by a remarkable resilience.

Revisiting Robben Island, Cape Town,
South Africa, February 11, 1994

The cell is an ideal place to learn to know yourself, to search realistically and regularly the process of your own mind and feelings.

From a letter to Winnie Mandela, then in Kroonstad Prison,
South Africa, written on Robben Island, February 1, 1975

The fact that you could sit alone and think gave us a wonderful opportunity to change ourselves.

From a BBC (UK) documentary, 1996

Writing a Letter in Prison

The utmost caution becomes particularly necessary where an autobiography is written clandestinely in prison, where one deals with political colleagues who themselves live under the hardships and tensions of prison life, who are in daily contact with officials who have a mania for persecuting prisoners.

From an unpublished autobiographical manuscript,
written on Robben Island, 1975

Writing is a prestigious profession which puts one right in the center of the world, and to remain on top, one has to work really hard, the aim being a good and original theme, simplicity in expression and the use of the irreplaceable word.

From a letter to Zindzi Mandela,
written on Robben Island, September 4, 1977

Writing a letter in prison can be a costly and frustrating exercise. Some of the letters are referred to the prison headquarters in Pretoria for approval, a process which invariably involves lengthy delays, at times stretching over several months. When the reply comes at long last it is usually a curt "not approved" and, as a general practice, no reasons whatsoever are given for the decision.

From a letter to Professor Samuel Dash,
written in Pollsmoor Prison, Cape Town,
South Africa, May 12, 1986

The False Image

I was planning to help correct the errors of South Africa and had forgotten that the first step in doing so was to overcome the weakness of the one South African I knew very well, myself.

From an unpublished autobiographical manuscript, written on Robben Island, 1975

One issue that deeply worried me in prison was the false image that I unwittingly projected to the outside world: of being regarded as a saint. I never was one, even on the basis of an earthly definition of a saint as a sinner who keeps on trying.

From the unpublished sequel to his autobiography, circa 1998

People expect me to perform far beyond my ability.

From an interview with John Battersby, Johannesburg, South Africa, published in the *Christian Science Monitor,* February 10, 2000

It is not at all correct to elevate any human being to the position of a god.

At home, Soweto, South Africa, February 1990

When I look back at some of my early writings and speeches I am appalled by their pedantry, artificiality and lack of originality. The urge to impress is clearly noticeable.

From a letter to Winnie Mandela,
written on Robben Island, June 20, 1970

I sometimes believe that through me creation intended to give the world the example of a mediocre man in the proper sense of the term.

From a letter to Fatima Meer,
written on Robben Island, March 1, 1971

A Virtually Widowed Woman

My main problem since I left home is my sleeping without you next to me and my waking up without you close to me, the passing of the day without my having seen you and with that audible voice of yours. The letters I write to you and those you write to me are an ointment to the wounds of our separation.

From a letter to Winnie Mandela,
written on Robben Island, October 26, 1976

It's been a valuable experience for me to watch powerful organizations and highly placed individuals clubbing together for the specific purpose of destroying a virtually widowed woman; how all these can stoop so low as to bring to my notice all sorts of details calculated to dim the clear image I have about the most wonderful friend I have in life completely baffles me.

From a letter to Winnie Mandela,
written on Robben Island, August 19, 1976

The question of my wife being harassed and persecuted by the police, and sometimes being assaulted, and I was not there to defend her. That was a very difficult moment for me.

From a conversation with Richard Stengel, March 9, 1993

I shall personally never regret the life Comrade Nomzamo [Winnie Mandela] and I tried to share together. Circumstances beyond our control, however, dictated it should be otherwise. I part from my wife with no recriminations. I embrace her with all the love and affection I have nursed for her inside and outside prison from the moment I first met her.

Announcing his separation from Winnie Mandela,
Johannesburg, South Africa, April 13, 1992

THE OPPRESSED AND THE OPPRESSOR ALIKE

I knew as well as I knew anything that the oppressor must be liberated just as surely as the oppressed. A man who takes away another man's freedom is a prisoner of hatred, he is locked behind the bars of prejudice and narrow-mindedness. I am not truly free if I am taking away someone else's freedom, just as sure as I am not free when my humanity is taken from me. The oppressed and the oppressor alike are robbed of their humanity.

From *Long Walk to Freedom,* 1994

Once you have rid yourself of the fear of the oppressor and his prisons, his police, his army, there is nothing that they can do. You are liberated.

From a conversation with Richard Stengel, March 9, 1993

It could have been that we inscribed vengeance on our banners of battle and resolved to meet brutality with brutality. But we understood that oppression dehumanizes the oppressor as it hurts the oppressed. We understood that to emulate the barbarity of the tyrant would also transform us into savages. We knew that we would sully and degrade our cause if we allowed that it should, at any stage, borrow anything from the practices of the oppressor. We had to refuse that our long sacrifice should make a stone of our hearts.

From a statement at the Parliament of the Republic of Ireland, Dublin, Ireland, July 2, 1990

Those who sought their own freedom in the domination of others were doomed in time to ignominious failure.

At the signing of the new Constitution, Sharpeville, Vereeniging, South Africa, December 10, 1996

THE NOBLE CHORUS

Every day we heard your voices ring—"Free the political prisoners!" We heard your voices sing—"Let my people go!" As we heard that vibrant and invigorating cry of human concern, we knew that we would be free.

Speaking at the Cathedral of Uppsala,
Uppsala, Sweden, March 13, 1990

We shall never forget how millions of people around the world joined us in solidarity to fight the injustice of our oppression while we were incarcerated.

Live 8 concert, Mary Fitzgerald Square,
Johannesburg, South Africa, July 2, 2005

In the end, the high and mighty also heard the voice of the little people. They too discovered that buried away in the dungeons of the Pretoria regime were men and women who should never have been arrested in the first place. They too joined the noble chorus—"free the political prisoners."

Speaking at the Cathedral of Uppsala,
Uppsala, Sweden, March 13, 1990

Part Two

VICTORY

Victory in a great cause is measured not only by reaching the final goal. It is also a triumph to live up to expectations in your lifetime.

From a letter to the Reverend Frank Chikane,
written in Victor Verster Prison,
Paarl, South Africa, August 21, 1989

I Greet You All in the Name of Peace

Friends, comrades and fellow South Africans, I greet you all in the name of peace, democracy and freedom for all! I stand here before you not as a prophet but as a humble servant of you, the people. Your tireless and heroic sacrifices have made it possible for me to be here today. I therefore place the remaining years of my life in your hands.

First speech after his release, City Hall,
Cape Town, South Africa, February 11, 1990

I am absolutely excited to be out.

First press conference after his release, Bishopscourt,
Archbishop Desmond Tutu's residence,
Cape Town, South Africa, February 12, 1990

Well I'm happy to be back home, it is a very rewarding and enriching experience to resume normal life and to hear the laughter of the children and to be able to guide them as they grow.

From an interview, circa 1993

After one has been in prison it is the small things that one appreciates—the feeling of being able to take a walk whenever one wants, to cross a road, to go into a shop and buy a newspaper, to speak or choose to remain silent—the simple act of being able to control one's person.

From a conversation with Ahmed Kathrada, circa 1993/94

The First Democratically Elected President

I, Nelson Rolihlahla Mandela, do hereby swear to devote myself to the well-being of the Republic of South Africa and all its people.

Oath of office, inauguration as President of South Africa, Union Buildings, Pretoria, South Africa, May 10, 1994

My installation as the first democratically elected president of the Republic of South Africa was imposed on me much against my advice.

From the unpublished sequel to his autobiography, circa 1998

Now the former terrorist had the task of uniting South Africa, of implementing the core principle of the Freedom Charter which declares that South Africa belongs to all its people, black and white.

From the unpublished sequel to his autobiography, circa 1998

THE FREEDOMS WHICH DEMOCRACY BRINGS

We were mindful from the very start of the importance of accountability to democracy. Our experience had made us acutely aware of the possible dangers of a government that is neither transparent nor accountable.

African Regional Workshop of the International Ombudsman Institute, Pretoria, South Africa, August 26, 1996

Let this, however, be clear: there is no place in a democracy for any community or section of a community to impose its will at the expense of the fundamental rights of any other citizen.

From an announcement of the election date, multi-party negotiations process, Kempton Park, South Africa, November 17, 1993

The freedoms which democracy brings will remain empty shells if they are not accompanied by real and tangible improvements in the material lives of millions of ordinary citizens of those countries.

From the documentary *Viva Madiba: A Hero for All Seasons,* 2010

People must be allowed to determine their own destiny.

At home, Soweto, South Africa, February 14, 1990

Compromise Is the Only Alternative

No problem is so deep that it cannot be overcome, given the will of all parties, through discussion and negotiation rather than force and violence.

From an address at the opening of the President's budget debate, Parliament, Cape Town, South Africa, March 2, 1999

In every dispute you eventually reach a point where neither party is altogether right or altogether wrong, when compromise is the only alternative for those who seriously want peace and stability.

From a personal file, January 16, 2000

If you don't intend having a compromise, you don't negotiate at all.

At home, Soweto, South Africa, February 14, 1990

Our experience has taught us that with goodwill a negotiated solution can be found for even the most profound problems.

Message for Jewish New Year (Rosh Hashanah),
South Africa, September 13, 1996

Our observation is that men and women throughout the world want peace, want security, want to get on with their lives and the very fact that parties that have been in conflict are sitting down to talk sends a message of hope to many people, not only in the area affected but throughout the world.

After meeting Sinn Fein leader Gerry Adams, Shell House,
Johannesburg, South Africa, June 19, 1995

Historical enemies succeeded in negotiating a peaceful transition from apartheid to democracy exactly because we were prepared to accept the inherent capacity for goodness in the other.

Joint sitting of Parliament to mark ten years of democracy, National
Assembly Parliament, Cape Town, South Africa, May 10, 2004

If You Are Negotiating

If you are negotiating you must do so in a spirit of reconciliation, not from the point of view of issuing ultimatums.

Addressing the media after meeting with
President F. W. de Klerk about violence on the East Rand,
Union Buildings, Cape Town, South Africa, circa early 1990s

I have discovered that in discussions it never helps to take a morally superior tone to one's opponent.

From *Long Walk to Freedom,* 1994

A softer approach, especially when you are confident of a case, brings about results far more than aggression.

From a conversation with Richard Stengel, February 8, 1993

The best weapon is to sit down and talk.

From the documentary *Mandela: The Living Legend,* 2003

Often, the most discouraging moments are precisely the time to launch an initiative. At such times, people are searching for a way out of their dilemma.

From *Long Walk to Freedom,* 1994

To Cast My First Vote

I waited for over seventy years to cast my first vote.

From the Bram Fischer Memorial Lecture, Market Theatre, Johannesburg,South Africa, June 9, 1995

I felt that with me when I voted were Oliver Tambo, Chris Hani, Chief Albert Luthuli and Bram Fischer. I felt that Josiah Gumede, G. M. Naicker, Dr. Abdullah Abdurahman, Lilian Ngoyi, Helen Joseph, Yusuf Dadoo, Moses Kotane, Steve Biko and many others were there. I felt that each one of them held my hand that made the cross, helped me to fold the ballot paper and push it into the ballot box.

From the Bram Fischer Memorial Lecture, Market Theatre, Johannesburg, South Africa, June 9, 1995

Standing on the sidelines, failing to go to the polls is a neglect of the democratic duty.

ANC election rally, FNB Stadium, Soweto, April 4, 2004

If anything symbolizes to the world the miracle of our transition, and earned us their admiration, it is the image of the patient queues of voters of April 1994 as South Africans in their millions, from every community and background, asserted their determination that, whatever the difficulties, the people shall govern so that we should never relive our experience of oppression, injustice and inhumanity.

From an address at the opening of the President's budget debate, Parliament, Cape Town, South Africa, March 2, 1999

I hope to have more years voting, and even if I go to the grave I will wake up and come and vote.

After voting, March 1, 2006

A Real Leader

I was backward politically and I was dealing with chaps, you see, who knew politics, who could discuss what was happening in South Africa and outside South Africa.

From a conversation with Richard Stengel, about his initial nervousness at participating in political meetings in the 1940s, March 16, 1993

Success in politics demands that you must take your people into confidence about your views and state them very clearly, very politely, very calmly, but nevertheless state them openly.

From a conversation with Richard Stengel, April 29, 1993

A real leader uses every issue, no matter how serious and sensitive, to ensure that at the end of the debate we should emerge stronger and more united than ever before.

From a personal notebook, January 16, 2000

We have had men who were so arrogant that they wanted to conquer the world and turn human beings into their slaves. But the people always put an end to such men and women.

From an address to Parliament of the World's Religions,
Cape Town, South Africa, December 1999

The trouble, of course, is that most successful men are prone to some form of vanity. There comes a stage in their lives when they consider it permissible to be egotistic and to brag to the public at large about their unique achievements.

From a letter to Fatima Meer,
written on Robben Island, March 1, 1971

Those who are in the center of political struggle, who have to deal with practical and pressing problems, are afforded little time for reflection and no precedents to guide them and are bound to slip up many times.

From an unpublished autobiographical manuscript,
written on Robben Island, 1975

We Chose Reconciliation

We were expected to destroy one another and ourselves collectively in the worst racial conflagration. Instead, we as a people chose the path of negotiation, compromise and peaceful settlement. Instead of hatred and revenge we chose reconciliation and nation-building.

Speaking at Nobel Square, Cape Town, South Africa,
December 14, 2003

The time for healing of the wounds has come. The moment to bridge the chasm that divides us has come. The time to build is upon us.

Inauguration as President of South Africa,
Union Buildings, Pretoria, South Africa, May 10, 1994

In the end, reconciliation is a spiritual process, which requires more than just a legal framework. It has to happen in the hearts and minds of people.

At the Annual Conference of the Methodist Church,
Mthatha, South Africa, September 18, 1994

Reconciliation means working together to correct the legacy of past injustice.

National Reconciliation Day, South Africa,
December 16, 1995

Reconciliation was not an afterthought or an add-on of our struggle and our eventual triumph. It was always imbedded in our struggle. Reconciliation was a means of struggle as much as it was the end goal of our struggle.

Speaking at a conference of the International Women's Forum,
Tokyo, Japan, January 30, 2003

We Have to Forgive the Past

We have to forgive the past but, at the same time, ensure that the dignity of the victims is restored, and their plight properly addressed.

At the Annual Conference of the Methodist Church,
Mthatha, South Africa, September 18, 1994

We recall our terrible past so that we can deal with it, to forgive where forgiveness is necessary, without forgetting, to ensure that never again will such inhumanity tear us apart and to move ourselves to eradicate a legacy that lurks dangerously as a threat to our democracy.

Special debate on the report of the TRC
(Truth and Reconciliation Commission), Parliament,
Cape Town, South Africa, February 25, 1999

I am working now with the same people who threw me into jail, persecuted my wife, hounded my children from one school to the other . . . and I am one of those who are saying, "Let us forget the past, and think of the present."

From a conversation with Richard Stengel, March 9, 1993

I Am Not Particularly Religious

Always make religion a personal and private affair confined to yourself. Do not burden others with your religious and other personal affairs.

From a letter to Makaziwe Mandela,
written on Robben Island, December 21, 1978

Religion, especially belief in the existence of a Supreme Being, has always been a controversial subject that splits nations and even families. But it is always best to treat the relationship between a man and his god as a purely personal affair, a question of faith and not of logic. No one has the right to prescribe to others what they should or should not believe in.

From a letter to Mrs. Deborah Opitz,
written in Pollsmoor Prison, Cape Town, South Africa, May 10, 1989

As with other aspects of its heritage, African traditional religion is increasingly recognized for its contribution to the world. No longer seen as despised superstition which had to be superseded by superior forms of belief: today its enrichment of humanity's spiritual heritage is acknowledged.

From a lecture at the Oxford Centre of Islamic Studies,
Sheldonian Theatre, Oxford, England, July 11, 1997

I am not particularly religious or spiritual. Let's say I am interested in all attempts to discover the meaning and purpose of life. Religion is an important part of this exercise.

From an interview with Charles Villa-Vicencio,
Johannesburg, South Africa, 1993

We Need Religious Institutions

We need religious institutions to continue to be the conscience of society, a moral custodian and a fearless champion of the interests of the weak and downtrodden. We need religious organizations to be part of a civil society mobilized to campaign for justice and the protection of basic human rights.

Regina Mundi Day, Regina Mundi Church,
Soweto, South Africa, November 30, 1997

The moral decay of some communities in various parts of the world reveals itself among others in the use of the name of God to justify the maintenance of actions which are condemned by the entire world as crimes against humanity.

From the unpublished sequel to his autobiography, circa 1998

Our religious leaders were in the forefront of keeping the spirit of resistance alive amongst our people in those days when repression intensified and took on horrendous proportions intended to cow the people into submission.

Seventy-fifth birthday of Archbishop Desmond Tutu,
Johannesburg, South Africa, October 8, 2006

Without the church, without religious institutions, I would never have been here today.

From an address to Parliament of the World's Religions,
Cape Town, South Africa, December 1999

OUR DIFFERENCES ARE OUR STRENGTH

There are good men and women in any community and in all political parties or persuasions. It is when those men and women get together that the builders rather than the destroyers triumph. It is then that our common humanity is reaffirmed.

Peace Festival, Centre Jeunes Kamenge,
Bujumbura, Burundi, December 2000

Our differences are our strength as a species and as a world community.

Upon receiving the Franklin D. Roosevelt
Four Freedoms Award, June 8, 2002

People, not only in our country but around the world, were inspired to believe that through common human effort, injustice can be overcome and that together a better life for all can be achieved.

From a letter to President Barack Obama on
the occasion of his inauguration, January 20, 2009

Part Three

WISDOM

The anchor of all my dreams is the collective wisdom of mankind as a whole.

From a letter to Senator Douglas Lukhele,
written on Robben Island, August 1, 1970

NONE OF US IS A SUPERSTAR

The important thing to remember is that no single person can do everything.

Father's Day lunch hosted by Zindzi Mandela,
Hyatt Women of Vision Club,
Johannesburg, South Africa, June 1, 2001

In Africa we have a concept known as ubuntu, based upon the recognition that we are only people because of other people.

Closing of the XIV International AIDS Conference,
Barcelona, Spain, July 12, 2002

None of us is a superstar and none can succeed without the success of the other.

OAU (Organization of African Unity) Summit,
Ouagadougou, Burkina Faso, June 8, 1998

PEACE IS THE GREATEST WEAPON

No serious political organization will ever talk peace when an aggressive war is being waged against it.

Cape Town, South Africa, date unknown

Peace is the greatest weapon for development that any people can have.

From an address to the National Executive Committee of Chama Cha Mapinduzi (ruling party of Tanzania), Dar es Salaam, Tanzania, November 17, 1998

All of us should ask ourselves the question: have I done everything in my power to bring about lasting peace and prosperity in my city and my country?

Upon receiving the Freedom of Durban, South Africa, April 16, 1999

Our strongest weapon which the enemy can never be able to resist is peace.

From a conversation with Ahmed Kathrada and Mac Maharaj,
Johannesburg, South Africa, July 27, 2006

It may well be that the days when nations will turn mighty armies into powerful peace movements, and deadly weapons into harmless ploughshares are still years away. But it is a source of real hope that there are today world organizations, governments, heads of state, influential groups and individuals who are striving earnestly and courageously for world peace.

From a letter to Lord Nicholas Bethell,
written in Pollsmoor Prison,
Cape Town, South Africa, June 4, 1986

There can be no greater cause in the world today than the quest for peace.

Johannesburg Press Club "Newsmaker of the Decade"
Gala Dinner, Johannesburg, South Africa, October 31, 2001

CHARACTER OF GROWTH

A good head and a good heart are always a formidable combination.

From a letter to Fatima Meer,
written on Robben Island, January 1, 1976

It is what we make out of what we have, not what we are given, that separates one person from another.

From *Long Walk to Freedom,* 1994

It is in the character of growth that we should learn from both pleasant and unpleasant experiences.

Foreign Correspondents Association annual dinner, Johannesburg, South Africa, November 21, 1997

Masters of Our Own Fate

Once a person is determined to help themselves, there is nothing that can stop them.

Father's Day lunch hosted by Zindzi Mandela,
Hyatt Women of Vision Club,
Johannesburg, South Africa, June 1, 2001

Blaming things on the past does not make them better.

Rolihlahla Primary School, Warrenton,
South Africa, August 30, 1996

I never think of the time I have lost. I just carry out a program because it's there. It's mapped out for me.

From a conversation with Richard Stengel, May 3, 1993

What matters is not so much what happens to a person than the way such person takes it.

From a letter to Tim Maharaj,
written on Robben Island, February 1, 1971

When you have got a program to apply, whatever the merits of that program, it is difficult to concentrate on the negative aspects of your life.

Revisiting Robben Island, South Africa, February 11, 1994

No longer shall we seek to place blame for our condition elsewhere or to look to others to take responsibility for our development. We are the masters of our own fate.

Banquet celebrating Africa's 100 best books of
the twentieth century, Cape Town, South Africa, July 2002

One of the most difficult things is not to change society—but to change yourself.

From an interview with John Battersby,
Johannesburg, South Africa, published in the
Christian Science Monitor, February 10, 2000

Turn Our Common Suffering into Hope

Our human compassion binds us the one to the other—not in pity or patronizingly, but as human beings who have learned how to turn our common suffering into hope for the future.

From a message to the Healing and Reconciliation Service "Dedicated to HIV/AIDS Sufferers and for the Healing of Our Land," December 6, 2000

Take it upon yourself where you live to make people around you joyful and full of hope.

At the opening of the Zola Clinic, Soweto, South Africa, March 7, 2002

Hope is a powerful weapon, and [one] no one power on earth can deprive you of.

From a letter to Winnie Mandela,
written on Robben Island, June 23, 1969

Who Are Full of Contradictions

In real life we deal, not with gods, but with ordinary humans like ourselves: men and women who are full of contradictions, who are stable and fickle, strong and weak, famous and infamous.

From a letter to Winnie Mandela,
written on Robben Island, December 9, 1979

The process of illusion and disillusionment is part of life and goes on endlessly.

From an unpublished autobiographical manuscript,
written on Robben Island, 1975

Contradictions are an essential part of life and never cease tearing one apart.

From an undated letter to Effie Schultz,
written in Pollsmoor Prison, Cape Town, South Africa, April 1, 1987

The Capacity of Memory

Until I was jailed I never fully appreciated the capacity of memory, the endless string of information the head can carry.

From a letter to Hilda Bernstein,
written in Pollsmoor Prison,
Cape Town, South Africa, July 8, 1985

In the life of any individual, family, community or society, memory is of fundamental importance. It is the fabric of identity.

From *A Prisoner in the Garden: Opening Nelson Mandela's Prison Archive*, 2005

Tested and Dependable Friends

The support of tested and dependable friends gives one the strength to hold on to hope and to endure successfully even the most challenging knocks in life.

From a letter to Don Mattera,
written in Victor Verster Prison,
Paarl, South Africa, April 4, 1989

Our morality does not allow us to desert our friends.

At a reception hosted by President Bill Clinton,
the White House, Washington DC, USA,
September 22, 1998

I have a special attachment to the people who befriended me during times of distress.

From an unpublished autobiographical manuscript, written on Robben Island, 1975

Rising Every Time You Fall

Disasters will always come and go, leaving their victims either completely broken or steeled and seasoned and better able to face the next crop of challenges that may occur.

From a letter to Winnie Mandela,
written on Robben Island, June 23, 1969

I am convinced that floods of personal disaster can never drown a determined revolutionary nor can the cumulus of misery that accompanies tragedy suffocate him.

From a letter to Winnie Mandela,
written on Robben Island, August 1, 1970

There are few misfortunes in this world that you cannot turn into a personal triumph if you have the iron will and the necessary skill.

From a letter to Zindzi Mandela
written on Robben Island, March 25, 1979

If our expectations—if our fondest prayers and dreams—are not realized, then we should all bear in mind that the greatest glory of living lies not in never falling, but in rising every time you fall.

At a reception hosted by President Bill Clinton,
the White House, Washington DC, USA,
September 22, 1998

I Have Stumbled

It will probably shock many people to discover how colossally ignorant I am about simple things the ordinary person takes for granted.

From a personal file, circa 1996

I didn't want to be presented in a way that omits the dark spots in my life.

From a conversation with Richard Stengel, March 16, 1993

I was arrogant [in] those days.

From a conversation about 1962 with
Ahmed Kathrada, circa 1993/94

On occasion, like other leaders, I have stumbled; and cannot claim to sparkle alone on a glorified perch.

From an article written for the *Sunday Times*
(South Africa), February 22, 1996

For Humanity to Produce Saints

Difficulties break some men but make others. No axe is sharp enough to cut the soul of a sinner who keeps on trying.

From a letter to Winnie Mandela,
written on Robben Island, February 1, 1975

Someday in the future it'll be possible for humanity to produce saints who will really be upright and venerable, inspired in everything they do by genuine love for humanity and who'll serve all humans selflessly.

From a letter to Winnie Mandela,
written on Robben Island, August 19, 1976

One may be a villain for three-quarters of his life and be canonized because he lived a holy life for the remaining quarter of that life.

From a letter to Winnie Mandela,
written on Robben Island, December 9, 1979

Never forget that a saint is a sinner who keeps on trying.

From a letter to Winnie Mandela,
written on Robben Island, February 1, 1975

NO POWER ON EARTH THAT CAN COMPARE

Religion is about mutual love and respect for one another and for life itself. It is about the dignity and equality of humankind made in the image of God.

From an interview with Charles Villa-Vicencio,
Johannesburg, South Africa, 1993

Belief in the possibility of change and renewal is perhaps one of the defining characteristics of politics and of religions.

From a lecture at the Oxford Centre of Islamic Studies,
Sheldonian Theatre, Oxford, England, July 11, 1997

The path of those who preach love, and not hatred, is not easy. They often have to wear a crown of thorns.

From a message to the Global Convention on Peace and Non-violence, New Delhi, India, January 31, 2004

There is no power on earth that can compare with religion, that's why I respect it.

From a BBC (UK) documentary, 1996

EDUCATION IS THE GREAT ENGINE

Education is the great engine of personal development. It is through education that the daughter of a peasant can become a doctor, that the son of a mineworker can become the head of the mine, that a child of farmworkers can become the president of a great nation. It is what we make out of what we have, not what we are given, that separates one person from another.

From *Long Walk to Freedom,* 1994

It is not beyond our power to create a world in which all children have access to a good education.

From a recorded message for the launch of the Nelson Mandela Institute for Education and Rural Development, November 2007

To work hard and systematically in your studies throughout the year, will in the end bring you coveted prizes and much personal happiness.

From a letter to Makgatho Mandela,
written on Robben Island, July 28, 1969

Education is the most powerful weapon we can use to change the world.

From an address at the Planetarium,
Johannesburg, South Africa, July 16, 2003

MY FAVORITE PASTIME

I was reading and I discovered that there was a world which I did not know, whose doors opened to me, and the influences of these men must be reckoned as against that background.

From a conversation with Richard Stengel, May 3, 1993

It is always a special pleasure to talk to children about my favorite pastime: reading.

Launch of *Madiba: The Rainbow Man,* November 27, 1997

One of the sad realities today is that very few people, especially young people, read books. Unless we can find imaginative ways of addressing this reality, future generations are in danger of losing their history.

Launch of the Izipho exhibition, book and
comic series, Nelson Mandela Foundation,
Johannesburg, South Africa, July 14, 2005

When you read works of that nature you become encouraged. It puts life in you.

From a conversation with Richard Stengel, about the poem "Invictus" (1875), by William Ernest Henley, circa March 1993

An autobiography is not merely a catalogue of events and experiences in which a person has been involved, but it also serves as some blueprint on which others may well model their own lives.

From the unpublished sequel to his autobiography, circa 1998

One of the things that made me long to be back in prison was that I had so little opportunity for reading, thinking and quiet reflection after my release.

From the "retiring from retirement" press conference, Nelson Mandela Foundation, Johannesburg, South Africa, June 2, 2004

I Speak of Culture

I speak of culture and creativity because, like truth, they are enduring.

Unveiling of a statue to mark the twentieth anniversary of the death of Steve Biko, East London, South Africa, September 1, 1997

I am proud of what I am, of my country and people, our history and tradition, language, music and art and firmly believe that Africans have something distinct to offer to world culture.

From an unpublished autobiographical manuscript, written on Robben Island, 1975

The rights of every citizen to his or her language, culture and religion must also be guaranteed.

From an address at the European Parliament, Strasbourg, France, June 13, 1990

We can only achieve that better life for ordinary people and citizens on our continent if we take seriously and give priority to those simple precepts of humanity that literature, good literature, always deals with. We can achieve that if we ensure that literature and the pursuits of the human spirit are taken seriously and accorded value in our society and our societal pursuits.

Banquet celebrating Africa's 100 best books of the twentieth century, Cape Town, South Africa, July 2002

AHEAD OF THE CHILDREN

I admire young people who are concerned with the affairs of their community and nation, perhaps because I also became involved in struggle whilst I was still at school. With such youth we can be sure that the ideals we celebrate today will never be extinguished. Young people are capable, when aroused, of bringing down the towers of oppression and raising the banners of freedom.

Anniversary of Bastille Day, Paris, France, July 14, 1996

This past century has seen more than its share of miseries and injustice amongst the peoples of the world but the younger generations being educated in our schools have every reason to expect a better world.

From a recorded message for the Round Square campaign,
South Africa, October 4, 1996

In a world that so often decries the apathy of its youth, we can open our arms for the millions of adolescents eager to contribute their new ideas and bounding enthusiasm.

From a statement on Building a
Global Partnership for Children, May 6, 2000

The struggle for true and universal human emancipation still lies ahead of the children, youth and future generations of our planet.

Launch of the Robert F. Wagner Graduate School
of Public Service, African Public Service Fellowship Fund,
New York University, New York City, USA, May 7, 2002

Just Because of Your Grey Hair

Let me restate the obvious: I have long passed my teens; and the distance to my final destination is shorter than the road I have trudged over the years! All of us have to live with this truth, without suffering undue insecurity. That is what nature has decreed.

From an article written for the *Sunday Times* (South Africa), February 22, 1996

One of the advantages of old age is that people respect you just because of your grey hair and say all manner of nice things about you that are not based on who you really are.

Eightieth birthday celebration, Gallagher estate, Midrand, South Africa, July 19, 1998

A society that does not value its older people denies its roots and endangers its future. Let us strive to enhance their capacity to support themselves for as long as possible and, when they cannot do so anymore, to care for them.

From a message announcing 1999 as the
United Nations International Year of Older Persons,
December 17, 1998

I am not sick, I'm old.

Johannesburg, South Africa, January 27, 2011

It Must Not Disturb My Hair

If there is anything I can boast about it is that I am taller than the President of the United States of America.

Referring to President Jimmy Carter
at the opening of the Zola Clinic,
Soweto, South Africa, March 7, 2002

It must not disturb my hair, I took an hour combing it.

Putting headphones on upside down,
from the documentary *Mandela: The Living Legend,* 2003

A rapidly increasing weight has induced me to cut out lunch and the afternoon snack.

From a letter to Brigadier Keulder, Commanding Officer,
written in Victor Verster Prison,
Paarl, South Africa, October 9, 1989

Every time I put on that thing I can't even talk. I find it difficult even to talk.

Talking to his assistants who want him to
wear a bowtie to the official inauguration dinner,
from a BBC (UK) documentary, 1996

SPORT HAS THE POWER TO CHANGE THE WORLD

Taking part in sports like running, swimming and tennis will keep you healthy, strong and bright.

From a letter to Dumani Mandela,
written in Victor Verster Prison, Paarl, South Africa,
February 28, 1989

Sport has the power to overcome old divisions and create the bond of common aspirations.

Banquet for the African Cup of Nations,
South Africa, March 1, 1996

Who could doubt that sport is a crucial window for the propagation of fair play and justice? After all, fair play is a value that is essential to sport!

Speaking at the International Fair Play Awards,
Pretoria, South Africa, June 25, 1997

Sport has the power to change the world. It has the power to inspire, it has the power to unite people in a way that little else does. It speaks to youth in a language they understand.

Receiving the inaugural Laureus Lifetime Achievement Award, Sporting Club, Monaco, Monte Carlo, May 25, 2000

Sport can create hope, where once there was only despair. It is more powerful than governments in breaking down racial barriers. It laughs in the face of all types of discrimination.

Receiving the inaugural Laureus Lifetime Achievement Award, Sporting Club, Monaco, Monte Carlo, May 25, 2000

There is one regret I have had throughout my life: that I never became the boxing heavyweight champion of the world.

Event with President Bill Clinton, Washington DC, USA, 1990

Being a Hero

It is so easy to break down and destroy. The heroes are those who make peace and build.

Sixth Annual Nelson Mandela Lecture, Walter Sisulu Square, Kliptown, Soweto, South Africa, July 12, 2008

For thousands of years and one generation after another, the human race has thrown up men and women of love, vision and boundless courage. It is thanks to these towering giants that our humanness has always remained with us and will always remain with us, no matter how difficult the challenges history throws at us from one historic era to another.

At the Anatomy of Hate: Resolving Conflict through Dialogue and Democracy International Conference, Oslo, Norway, August 26, 1990

Well, it's a nice feeling for people to talk of you in terms of being a hero. This is not really directed at me. I am used as a peg on which to hang all the adulation.

From the documentary *Viva Madiba: A Hero for All Seasons*, 2010

A STREAK OF GOODNESS

I would venture to say that there is something inherently good in all human beings, deriving from, among other things, the attribute of social consciousness that we all possess. And, yes, there is also something inherently bad in all of us, flesh and blood as we are, with the attendant desire to perpetuate and pamper the self.

Peace lecture of the World Conference on Religion and Peace (South African Chapter), Durban, South Africa, August 7, 1994

The simple lesson of all religions, of all philosophies and of life itself is that, although evil may be on the rampage temporarily, the good must win the laurels in the end.

From a letter to Fatima Meer, written on Robben Island, January 1, 1976

We accord persons dignity by assuming that they are good, that they share the human qualities we ascribe to ourselves.

Joint sitting of Parliament to mark ten years of democracy, Parliament, Cape Town, South Africa, May 10, 2004

In a cynical world we have become an inspiration to many. We signal that good can be achieved amongst human beings who are prepared to trust, prepared to believe in the goodness of people.

Joint sitting of Parliament to mark ten years of democracy, Parliament, Cape Town, South Africa, May 10, 2004

There is a streak of goodness in men that can be buried or hidden and then emerge unexpectedly.

From *Long Walk to Freedom,* 1994

What Difference We Have Made

It is in your hands to create a better world for all who live in it. Mandela Day will not be a holiday but a day devoted to service.

Nelson Mandela Foundation,
Johannesburg, South Africa, June 30, 2009

We tried in our simple way to lead our life in a manner that may make a difference to those of others.

Upon receiving the Franklin D. Roosevelt
Four Freedoms Award, June 8, 2002

What counts in life is not the mere fact that we have lived. It is what difference we have made to the lives of others that will determine the significance of the life we lead.

Ninetieth birthday celebration of Walter Sisulu,
Walter Sisulu Hall, Randburg, Johannesburg, South Africa,
May 18, 2002

No One Is Born Hating Another Person

No one is born hating another person because of the color of his skin, or his background, or his religion. People must learn to hate, and if they can learn to hate, they can be taught to love, for love comes more naturally to the human heart than its opposite.

From *Long Walk to Freedom,* 1994

People are human beings, produced by the society in which they live. You encourage people by seeing the good in them.

From an interview, date unknown

On which aspect one concentrates in judging others will depend on the character of the particular judge. As we judge others so we are judged by others.

From a letter to Winnie Mandela,
written on Robben Island, December 9, 1979

You have to recognize that people are produced by the mud in the society in which you live and that therefore they are human beings. They have got good points, they have got weak points. Your duty is to work with human beings as human beings, not because you think they are angels.

From a conversation with Richard Stengel, April 29, 1993

All men, even the most seemingly cold-blooded, have a core of decency, and if their hearts are touched, they are capable of changing.

From *Long Walk to Freedom,* 1994

We always think that others have got horns before you actually meet them.

After a visit with Betsie Verwoerd,
Orania, South Africa, August 15, 1995

Preparing a Master Plan

Significant progress is always possible if we ourselves try to plan every detail of our lives and actions and allow the intervention of fate only on our own terms.

From a letter to Thorobetsane Tshukudu
(Adelaide Tambo), written on Robben Island,
January 1, 1977

Preparing a master plan and applying it are two different things.

From an essay titled
"Whither the Black Consciousness Movement,"
written on Robben Island, 1978

At the beginning of the year, I used to take resolutions that this is what I would do, then I find that I can't even stick to that resolution for two days.

From a conversation with Richard Stengel, May 3, 1993

It is easy to make promises but never go to action.

Live 8 concert, Mary Fitzgerald Square,
Johannesburg, South Africa, July 2, 2005

I must be satisfied with my life as it is.

From the documentary *Mandela: The Living Legend,* 2003

WE HAVE LEARNED THE LESSON

We have learned the lesson that our blemishes speak of what all humanity should not do. We understand this fully that our glories point to the heights of what human genius can achieve.

First State of the Nation address, Parliament,
Cape Town, South Africa, May 24, 1994

I am also here today as a representative of the millions of people across the globe, the anti-apartheid movement, the governments and organizations that joined with us, not to fight against South Africa as a country or any of its peoples, but to oppose an inhuman system and pursue a speedy end to the apartheid crime against humanity.

Nobel Peace Prize award ceremony, Oslo, Norway, December 10, 1993

We have been forced to adopt sanctions because it was the only way, apart from the armed struggle, in which there can be movement forward.

At home, Soweto, South Africa, February 14, 1990

Great anger and violence can never build a nation.

Speaking at a rally, Kings Park Stadium,
Durban, South Africa, February 25, 1990

Out of the experience of an extraordinary human disaster that lasted too long, must be born a society of which all humanity will be proud.

Inauguration as President of South Africa,
Union Buildings, Pretoria, South Africa, May 10, 1994

The Time Has Come for Me to Take Leave

I have reached that part of the long walk when the opportunity is granted, as it should be to all men and women, to retire to some rest and tranquility in the village of my birth.

Fifty-third United Nations General Assembly, United Nations, New York City, USA, September 21, 1998

I don't want to reach 100 years whilst I am still trying to bring about a solution in some complicated international issue.

From a farewell briefing to editors and opinion makers, Pretoria, South Africa, May 10, 1999

Just remember I am looking for a job.

Joking to journalists about being unemployed, Johannesburg, South Africa, April 1, 2006

Thank you for being kind to an old man—allowing him to take a rest, even if many of you may feel that after loafing somewhere on an island and other places for twenty-seven years, the rest is not really deserved.

Upon "retiring from retirement," Nelson Mandela Foundation, Johannesburg, South Africa, June 1, 2004

The time has come for me to take leave. The time has come to hand over the baton in a relay that started more than eighty-five years ago.

Closing session of the fiftieth National Conference of the ANC, North-West University, Mafikeng Campus, South Africa, December 20, 1997

It was a matter of great comfort and consolation to me when the very young Bill Clinton joined me in the ranks of retired and discarded former presidents, now without office or power.

From a pre-recorded message to the Clinton Foundation, March 1, 2004

PART FOUR

FUTURE

The long walk continues.

Final sitting of the first democratically elected Parliament,
Cape Town, South Africa, March 26, 1999

It Was My Duty

The knowledge that in your day you did your duty, and lived up to the expectations of your fellow men is in itself a rewarding experience and magnificent achievement.

From a letter to Sheena Duncan, written in Pollsmoor Prison, Cape Town, South Africa, April 1, 1985

There was no particular day on which I said, henceforth I will devote myself to the liberation of my people; instead, I simply found myself doing so, and could not do otherwise.

From *Long Walk to Freedom,* 1994

If I had to live again I would do exactly the same thing. As long as our people were oppressed and deprived of everything to make human beings happy and to enjoy life, it was my duty to be involved and I'd do it all over and over again.

From the documentary *Mandela: The Living Legend,* 2003

The call now is for each of us to ask ourselves: are we doing all we can to help build the country of our dreams?

Intercultural Eid celebration, Johannesburg, South Africa, January 30, 1998

The Future Belongs to Our Youth

It is up to the youth to decisively and finally break our society out of the constricting and divisive definitions of our past.

Re-burial ceremony for Anton Lembede,
Mbumbulu, South Africa, October 27, 2002

To the youth of today, I also have a wish to make: be the script-writers of your destiny and feature yourselves as stars.

Birthday celebration for the Nelson Mandela Children's Fund,
French International School, Johannesburg, South Africa,
July 9, 2008

The display of leadership by our youth today gives me a comfort that not all is lost.

Birthday celebration for the Nelson Mandela Children's Fund,
French International School, Johannesburg, South Africa,
July 9, 2008

The future belongs to our youth. As some of us near the end of our political careers, younger people must take over. They must seek and cherish the most basic condition for peace, namely unity in our diversity, and find lasting ways to that goal.

Upon receiving an honorary doctorate,
University of Kwazulu-Natal, South Africa,
May 30, 1998

The Only Basis of Human Happiness

I am influenced more than ever before by the conviction that social equality is the only basis of human happiness.

From a letter to Senator Douglas Lukhele,
written on Robben Island, August 1, 1970

It has to be a better world: one in which the rights of every individual are respected, one that builds on past aspirations for a good life, and one that enables every individual to optimally develop their potential.

From a message to the World Social Forum,
Mumbai, India, January 2004

We must ensure that color, race and gender become only a God-given gift to each one of us and not an indelible mark or attribute that accords a special status to any.

Forty-ninth session of the United Nations General Assembly, New York City, USA, October 2, 1994

A nation should not be judged by how it treats its highest citizens, but its lowest ones.

From *Long Walk to Freedom*, 1994

AIDS Is No Longer Just a Disease

The more we lack the courage and the will to act, the more we condemn to death our brothers and sisters, our children and our grandchildren. When the history of our times is written, will we be remembered as the generation that turned our backs in a moment of global crisis or will it be recorded that we did the right thing?

46664 concert, Tromso, Norway, June 11, 2005

We need to break the silence, banish stigma and discrimination, and ensure total inclusiveness within the struggle against AIDS; those who are infected with this terrible disease do not want stigma, they want love.

Closing address at the XIII International AIDS Conference,
Durban, South Africa, July 14, 2000

AIDS is no longer just a disease: it is a human rights issue.

46664 concert, Green Point Stadium,
Cape Town, South Africa, November 29, 2003

We are all human, and the HIV/AIDS epidemic affects us all in the end. If we discard people who are dying from AIDS, then we can no longer call ourselves people.

Closing ceremony of the XIV International AIDS Conference,
Barcelona, Spain, July 12, 2002

My son has died of AIDS.

Press conference announcing the death of his son Makgatho
of AIDS, Johannesburg, South Africa, January 6, 2005

The Eradication of Poverty

Abject poverty is demeaning, is an assault on the dignity of those that suffer it. In the end it demeans us all. It makes the freedom of all of us less meaningful.

Upon receiving the Freedom Award from the National Civil Rights Museum, Memphis, Tennessee, USA, November 22, 2000

Poverty and material inequality are enemies of lasting peace and stability.

Closing session of the fiftieth National Conference of the ANC, North-West University, Mafikeng Campus, South Africa, December 20, 1997

A secure future for humanity depends as much as anything else on the rapid narrowing of the gap between the rich and the poor within single nations and amongst nations.

Twenty-sixth International Conference on
Improving University Teaching,
University of Johannesburg,
Johannesburg, South Africa, July 2001

We need to place the eradication of poverty at the top of world priorities. We need to know with a fresh conviction that we all share a common humanity and that our diversity in the world is the strength for our future together.

Banquet celebrating Africa's 100 best books of
the twentieth century, Cape Town, South Africa, July 2002

Where poverty exists, there is not true freedom.

Launch of the "Make Poverty History" campaign,
Trafalgar Square, London, England, February 3, 2005

Trapped in the Prison of Poverty

Jobs, jobs and jobs are the dividing line in many families between a decent life and a wretched existence. They are, to many, the difference between self-esteem and helplessness.

President's budget debate, Parliament, Cape Town, South Africa, June 20, 1996

To be poor is a terrible thing.

From a conversation with Ahmed Kathrada, circa 1993/94

Like slavery and apartheid, poverty is not natural. It is man-made and it can be overcome and eradicated by the actions of human beings.

Launch of the "Make Poverty History" campaign,
Trafalgar Square, London, England, February 3, 2005

In this new century, millions of people in the world's poorest countries remain imprisoned, enslaved and in chains. They are trapped in the prison of poverty. It is time to set them free.

Launch of the "Make Poverty History" campaign,
Trafalgar Square, London, England, February 3, 2005

Overcoming poverty is not a gesture of charity. It is an act of justice. It is the protection of a fundamental human right, the right to dignity and a decent life.

Live 8 concert, Mary Fitzgerald Square,
Johannesburg, South Africa, July 2, 2005

The Role and Place of Women

Freedom cannot be achieved unless the women have been emancipated from all forms of oppression.

First State of the Nation address, Parliament,
Cape Town, South Africa, May 24, 1994

No longer are we allowed to put the national question above gender issues; in fact, we are no longer allowed to think of the national question as something apart from the role and place of women in society.

Speaking at a dinner celebrating Women's Month,
Johannesburg Country Club, Johannesburg, South Africa,
August 25, 2003

I've never regarded women as in any way less competent than men.

From a letter to Advocate Felicity Kentridge, written on Robben Island, May 9, 1976

Criticism Is Necessary for Any Society

The question of surrounding yourself, both in structures and in your individual work, with people who are strong and who will resist if you do something wrong is really something worthwhile.

At the opening of ANC/Inkatha Freedom Summit,
Durban, South Africa, January 29, 1991

We know too well from our past experiences that robust and honest exchange of opinions and criticism is necessary for any society to be truly democratic and for any government to stay on course.

Luncheon hosted by the Conference of Editors,
South Africa, September 6, 1994

No single person, no body of opinion, no political doctrine, no religious doctrine can claim a monopoly on truth.

Address to the International Federation of Newspaper Publishers, Prague, Czech Republic, May 26, 1992

An educated, enlightened and informed population is one of the surest ways of promoting the health of a democracy.

St John's College, Johannesburg, South Africa, October 6, 2003

In human affairs, no single person, organization or social formation ever has a final or an absolutely correct position. It is through conversation, debate and critical discussion that we approach positions that may provide workable solutions.

Message to the eighth national COSATU (Congress of South African Trade Unions), Midrand, South Africa, September 15–18, 2003

A Culture of Caring

A fundamental concern for others in our individual and community lives would go a long way in making the world the better place we so passionately dreamt of.

Sixth Nelson Mandela Annual Lecture,
Kliptown, Soweto, South Africa, July 12, 2008

There can be no greater gift than that of giving one's time and energy to help others without expecting anything in return.

A ceremony to acknowledge FCB Harlow Butler Pty (Ltd.)
for supporting the Nelson Mandela Foundation's HIV/AIDS
and education programs, speaking at the
Nelson Mandela Foundation,
Johannesburg, South Africa,
February 27, 2004

Human beings regard their mental capacity as the most defining feature of themselves as a species. To respond in a caring manner to the impairment of those capacities in others is to really know ourselves as human beings and to live out our humanness.

Address at a fund-raising event for the Takalani Home
for the Mentally Disabled, Sparrow Schools and
Living Link, South Africa, September 2002

Our society needs to re-establish a culture of caring.

Father's Day lunch hosted by Zindzi Mandela,
Hyatt Women of Vision Club,
Johannesburg, South Africa, June 1, 2001

THE FOUNDATION OF ONE'S SPIRITUAL LIFE

Spiritual weapons can be dynamic and often have an impact difficult to appreciate except in the light of actual experience in given situations. In a way they make prisoners free men, turn commoners into monarchs and dirt into pure gold.

From a letter to Senator Douglas Lukhele,
written on Robben Island, August 1, 1970

There is universal respect and even admiration for those who are humble and simple by nature, and who have absolute confidence in all human beings irrespective of their social status.

From the unpublished sequel to his autobiography, circa 1998

In judging our progress as individuals we tend to concentrate on external factors such as one's social position, influence and popularity, wealth and standard of education. These are, of course, important in measuring one's success in material matters and it is perfectly understandable if many people exert themselves mainly to achieve all these. But internal factors may be even more crucial in assessing our development as a human being. Honesty, sincerity, simplicity, humility, pure generosity, absence of vanity, readiness to serve others—qualities which are within easy reach of every soul—are the foundation of one's spiritual life.

From a letter to Winnie Mandela,
written on Robben Island, February 1, 1975

Human Rights Are Ingrained

You must continue to promote the principle of relentless freedom and democracy, as it is the foundation upon which issues of human rights are ingrained.

From a video message for the National Youth Festival,
South Africa, June 2008

To deny people their human rights is to challenge their very humanity. To impose on them a wretched life of hunger and deprivation is to dehumanize them.

From an address to a joint session of the Houses of Congress,
Washington DC, USA, June 26, 1990

The basic human rights for all our citizens have to be protected and guaranteed, to ensure the genuine liberty of every individual.

Business Leadership Meeting, World Trade Center,
New York City, USA, June 21, 1990

As I am former prisoner number 46664, there is a special place in my heart for all those that are denied access to their basic human rights.

Closing ceremony of the XV International AIDS Conference,
Bangkok, Thailand, July 16, 2004

The mission of meaningful freedom, democracy and human rights is yet to be fulfilled.

From an address at the closing of the President's budget debate,
Parliament, Cape Town, South Africa, April 22, 1998

NO COUNTRY HOWEVER POWERFUL

No country, however powerful it may be, is entitled to act outside the United Nations. The United Nations was established in order that countries, irrespective of the continent from which they come, should act through an organized and disciplined body. The United Nations is here to promote peace in the world, and any country that acts outside the United Nations is making a serious mistake.

Press Conference, Jakarta, Indonesia, September 30, 2002

If there is a country that has committed unspeakable atrocities in the world, it is the United States of America.

Speaking at a conference of the International Women's Forum,
Tokyo, Japan, January 30, 2003

I have taken issue with the American political leadership where I thought they were acting contrary to the best values in American life and the American Constitution. For example, I strongly opposed the unilateral action taken outside of the United Nations with regards to Iraq. This has, however, not diminished my respect for America's leadership role in the world or my appreciation for the role its leaders play in the world.

Milton S. Eisenhower Symposium, Johns Hopkins University,
Baltimore, USA, November 12, 2003

I think the United States has become drunk with power.

From the documentary *Mandela: The Living Legend,* 2003

THE KEEPER OF OUR BROTHER AND SISTER

These countless human beings, both inside and outside our country, had the nobility of spirit to stand in the path of tyranny and injustice, without seeking selfish gain. They recognized that an injury to one is an injury to all.

Nobel Peace Prize award ceremony, Oslo, Norway, December 10, 1993

We are in this modern globalized world each the keeper of our brother and sister. We have too often failed that moral calling.

British Red Cross Humanity Lecture, Queen Elizabeth II Conference Centre, London, England, July 10, 2003

If a ninety-year-old may offer some unsolicited advice on this occasion, it would be that you, irrespective of your age, should place human solidarity, the concern for the other, at the center of the values by which you live.

Sixth Nelson Mandela Annual Lecture,
Kliptown, Soweto, South Africa, July 12, 2008

The values of human solidarity that once drove our quest for a humane society seem to have been replaced, or are being threatened, by a crass materialism and pursuit of social goals of instant gratification. One of the challenges of our time, without being pietistic or moralistic, is to re-instill in the consciousness of our people that sense of human solidarity, of being in the world for one another and because of and through others.

Fifth Steve Biko Lecture, University of Cape Town,
Cape Town, South Africa, September 10, 2004

All Parts of Our Planet

I do not like killing any living thing, even those creatures that fill some people with dread.

From *Long Walk to Freedom,* 1994

The streams of my youth that were places of beauty and inspiration were now clogged up and dirty. I saw the descendants of the mothers of our people bowing down to secure with their bare hands the cleanest of the dirty and dangerous water in those streams and pools.

Upon receiving the Planet and Humanity Award,
International Geographical Union,
Durban, South Africa, August 4, 2002

Our future as human beings depends on our intelligent and prudent use of the oceans. And that in turn will depend on the determined efforts of dedicated women and men from all parts of our planet.

Fifth session of the Independent World Commission
on the Oceans, Cape Town, South Africa,
November 11, 1997

Let us stand together to make of our world a sustainable source for our future as humanity on this planet.

Upon receiving the Planet and Humanity Award,
International Geographical Union,
Durban, South Africa, August 4, 2002

DEFY TODAY'S MERCHANTS OF CYNICISM

We shall take not just small steps, but giant leaps to a bright future in the new millennium. As we confounded the prophets of doom, we shall defy today's merchants of cynicism and despair.

State of the Nation address, Parliament,
Cape Town, South Africa, February 5, 1999

Sometimes it falls upon a generation to be great. You can be that great generation. Let your greatness blossom.

Launch of the "Make Poverty History" campaign,
Trafalgar Square, London, England, February 3, 2005

THE ONLY ROAD OPEN

Bridge the chasm, use tolerance and compassion, be inclusive not exclusive, build dignity and pride, encourage freedom of expression to create a civil society for unity and peace.

Opening of the cultural development congress at the Civic Theatre,
Johannesburg, South Africa, April 25, 1993

Let tolerance for one another's views create the peaceful conditions which give space for the best in all of us to find expression and to flourish.

At the signing of the new Constitution,
Sharpeville, Vereeniging, South Africa, December 10, 1996

We can build a society grounded on friendship and our common humanity—a society founded on tolerance. That is the only road open to us. It is a road to a glorious future in this beautiful country of ours. Let us join hands and march into the future.

From an announcement of the election date,
multi-party negotiations process,
Kempton Park, South Africa, November 17, 1993

It is the task of a new generation to lead and take responsibility; ours has done as well as it could in its time.

From a message at the launch of the ANC Election Manifesto
and ninety-seventh anniversary celebrations,
Absa Stadium, East London, South Africa,
January 10, 2009

A Bright Future Beckons

Will future generations say of us: "Indeed, they did lay the foundations for the eradication of world poverty; they succeeded in establishing a new world order based on mutual respect, partnership and equity"?

From a lecture at the Oxford Centre of Islamic Studies, Sheldonian Theatre, Oxford, England, July 11, 1997

Can we say with confidence that it is within our reach to declare that never again shall continents, countries or communities be reduced to the smoking battlefields of contending forces of nationality, religion, race or language? Shall we rise to the challenge which history has put before us, of ensuring that the world's prodigious capacity for economic growth benefits all its people and not just the powerful?

From a lecture at the Oxford Centre of Islamic Studies, Sheldonian Theatre, Oxford, England, July 11, 1997

Let it never be said by future generations that indifference, cynicism or selfishness made us fail to live up to the ideals of humanism which the Nobel Peace Prize encapsulates. Let the strivings of us all prove Martin Luther King Jr. to have been correct, when he said that humanity can no longer be tragically bound to the starless midnight of racism and war.

Nobel Peace Prize award ceremony, Oslo, Norway, December 10, 1993

A bright future beckons. The onus is on us, through hard work, honesty and integrity, to reach for the stars.

At the Freedom Day celebrations,
Pretoria, South Africa, April 27, 1996

Nobel Peace Prize Acceptance Speech, 1993

Your Majesty the King, Your Royal Highness, Esteemed Members of the Norwegian Nobel Committee, Honorable Prime Minister, Madam Gro Harlem Brundtland, Ministers, Members of Parliament and Ambassadors, Fellow Laureate, Mr. F. W. de Klerk, Distinguished Guests, Friends, Ladies and Gentlemen,

I extend my heartfelt thanks to the Norwegian Nobel Committee for elevating us to the status of a Nobel Peace Prize winner.

I would also like to take this opportunity to congratulate my compatriot and fellow laureate, State President F. W. de Klerk, on his receipt of this high honor.

Together, we join two distinguished South Africans, the late Chief Albert Luthuli and His Grace Archbishop Desmond Tutu, to whose seminal contributions to the peaceful struggle against the evil system of apartheid you paid well-deserved tribute by awarding them the Nobel Peace Prize.

It will not be presumptuous of us if we also add, among our predecessors, the name of another outstanding Nobel Peace Prize winner, the late Rev. Martin Luther King Jr.

He, too, grappled with and died in the effort to make a contribution to the just solution of the same great issues of the day which we have had to face as South Africans.

We speak here of the challenge of the dichotomies of war and peace, violence and non-violence, racism and human dignity, oppression and repression and liberty and human rights, poverty and freedom from want.

We stand here today as nothing more than a representative of the millions of our people who dared to rise up against a social system whose very essence is war, violence, racism, oppression, repression and the impoverishment of an entire people.

I am also here today as a representative of the millions of people across the globe, the anti-apartheid movement, the governments and organizations that joined with us, not to fight against South Africa as a country or any of its peoples, but to oppose an inhuman system and sue for a speedy end to the apartheid crime against humanity.

These countless human beings, both inside and outside our country, had the nobility of spirit to stand in the path of tyranny and injustice, without seeking selfish gain. They recognized that an injury to one is an injury to all and therefore acted together in defense of justice and a common human decency.

Because of their courage and persistence for many years,

we can, today, even set the dates when all humanity will join together to celebrate one of the outstanding human victories of our century.

When that moment comes, we shall, together, rejoice in a common victory over racism, apartheid and white minority rule.

That triumph will finally bring to a close a history of five hundred years of African colonization that began with the establishment of the Portuguese empire.

Thus, it will mark a great step forward in history and also serve as a common pledge of the peoples of the world to fight racism, wherever it occurs and whatever guise it assumes.

At the southern tip of the continent of Africa, a rich reward in the making, an invaluable gift is in the preparation for those who suffered in the name of all humanity when they sacrificed everything—for liberty, peace, human dignity and human fulfillment.

This reward will not be measured in money. Nor can it be reckoned in the collective price of the rare metals and precious stones that rest in the bowels of the African soil we tread in the footsteps of our ancestors.

It will and must be measured by the happiness and welfare of the children, at once the most vulnerable citizens in any society and the greatest of our treasures.

The children must, at last, play in the open veld, no longer tortured by the pangs of hunger or ravaged by disease or threatened with the scourge of ignorance, molestation and abuse, and no longer required to engage in deeds whose gravity exceeds the demands of their tender years.

In front of this distinguished audience, we commit the new

South Africa to the relentless pursuit of the purposes defined in the World Declaration on the Survival, Protection and Development of Children.

The reward of which we have spoken will and must also be measured by the happiness and welfare of the mothers and fathers of these children, who must walk the earth without fear of being robbed, killed for political or material profit, or spat upon because they are beggars.

They too must be relieved of the heavy burden of despair which they carry in their hearts, born of hunger, homelessness and unemployment.

The value of that gift to all who have suffered will and must be measured by the happiness and welfare of all the people of our country, who will have torn down the inhuman walls that divide them.

These great masses will have turned their backs on the grave insult to human dignity which described some as masters and others as servants, and transformed each into a predator whose survival depended on the destruction of the other.

The value of our shared reward will and must be measured by the joyful peace which will triumph, because the common humanity that bonds both black and white into one human race, will have said to each one of us that we shall all live like the children of paradise.

Thus shall we live, because we will have created a society which recognizes that all people are born equal, with each entitled in equal measure to life, liberty, prosperity, human rights and good governance.

Such a society should never allow again that there should be prisoners of conscience nor that any person's human rights should be violated.

Neither should it ever happen that once more the avenues to peaceful change are blocked by usurpers who seek to take power away from the people, in pursuit of their own, ignoble purposes.

In relation to these matters, we appeal to those who govern Burma that they release our fellow Nobel Peace Prize laureate, Aung San Suu Kyi, and engage her and those she represents in serious dialogue, for the benefit of all the people of Burma.

We pray that those who have the power to do so will, without further delay, permit that she uses her talents and energies for the greater good of the people of her country and humanity as a whole.

Far from the rough and tumble of the politics of our own country, I would like to take this opportunity to join the Norwegian Nobel Committee and pay tribute to my joint laureate. Mr. F. W. de Klerk.

He had the courage to admit that a terrible wrong had been done to our country and people through the imposition of the system of apartheid.

He had the foresight to understand and accept that all the people of South Africa must through negotiations and as equal participants in the process, together determine what they want to make of their future.

But there are still some within our country who wrongly believe they can make a contribution to the cause of justice and peace by clinging to the shibboleths that have been proved to spell nothing but disaster.

It remains our hope that these, too, will be blessed with sufficient reason to realize that history will not be denied and that the new society cannot be created by reproducing the repugnant past, however refined or enticingly repackaged.

We would also like to take advantage of this occasion to pay tribute to the many formations of the democratic movement of our country, including the members of our Patriotic Front, who have themselves played a central role in bringing our country as close to the democratic transformation as it is today.

We are happy that many representatives of these formations, including people who have served or are serving in the "homeland" structures, came with us to Oslo. They too must share the accolade which the Nobel Peace Prize confers.

We live with the hope that as she battles to remake herself, South Africa will be like a microcosm of the new world that is striving to be born.

This must be a world of democracy and respect for human rights, a world freed from the horrors of poverty, hunger, deprivation and ignorance, relieved of the threat and the scourge of civil wars and external aggression and unburdened of the great tragedy of millions forced to become refugees.

The processes in which South Africa and Southern Africa as a whole are engaged, beckon and urge us all that we take this tide at the flood and make of this region a living example of what all people of conscience would like the world to be.

We do not believe that this Nobel Peace Prize is intended as a commendation for matters that have happened and passed.

We hear the voices which say that it is an appeal from all

those, throughout the universe, who sought an end to the system of apartheid.

We understand their call, that we devote what remains of our lives to the use of our country's unique and painful experience to demonstrate, in practice, that the normal condition for human existence is democracy, justice, peace, non-racism, non-sexism, prosperity for everybody, a healthy environment and equality and solidarity among the peoples.

Moved by that appeal and inspired by the eminence you have thrust upon us, we undertake that we too will do what we can to contribute to the renewal of our world so that none should, in future, be described as the "wretched of the earth."

Let it never be said by future generations that indifference, cynicism or selfishness made us fail to live up to the ideals of humanism which the Nobel Peace Prize encapsulates.

Let the strivings of us all, prove Martin Luther King Jr. to have been correct, when he said that humanity can no longer be tragically bound to the starless midnight of racism and war.

Let the efforts of us all, prove that he was not a mere dreamer when he spoke of the beauty of genuine brotherhood and peace being more precious than diamonds or silver or gold.

Let a new age dawn!

Thank you.

ACKNOWLEDGMENTS

The Nelson Mandela Foundation Centre of Memory would like to acknowledge Nelson Rolihlahla Mandela for his wise words throughout his long and rich life: for the wisdom they bestow, the bravery they inspire, and the warmth they impart.

The Nelson Mandela Foundation Centre of Memory has provided a platform for work centered on the life and times and legacy of Nelson Mandela, and by doing so it has created the space for, among other projects, the creation of books such as this one. In this regard, thanks are due to the chairman of the Board of the Nelson Mandela Foundation, Professor GJ Gerwel; to the Board of Trustees of the Nelson Mandela Foundation—Ahmed Kathrada, Chris Liebenberg, Irene Menell, Kgalema Motlanthe, and Tokyo Sexwale; and to the chief executive of the Nelson Mandela Foundation, Achmat Dangor.

Verne Harris heads the Centre of Memory; it was his support that created the opportunity for this book to be published. If it were not for the enthusiasm and energy of Geoff Blackwell and Ruth Hobday of PQ Blackwell, this collection would not have seen the light of day.

Our team members in the Centre of Memory have also provided essential support. They are Lee Davies, Boniswa Nyati, Lucia Raadschelders, Zanele Riba, and Razia Saleh. Our colleagues Yase Godlo, Zelda la Grange, Thoko Mavuso, Vimla Naidoo, and Maretha Slabbert provided invaluable assistance.

We would also like to extend our gratitude to Ahmed Kathrada and Richard Stengel for donating to us many hours of recorded interviews with Mandela (made in the course of producing his autobiography *Long Walk to Freedom* and Anthony Sampson's *Mandela: The Authorised Biography*), and to the South African National Archives as well.

We are also grateful to Rachel Clare, Sarah Anderson, Anant Singh, and Nilesh Singh, and to Dr PR Anderson, Jennifer Pogrund, Anton Swart, Kerry Harris, Gail Behrmann, John Battersby, Professor Charles Villa-Vicencio, and Beata Lipman.

The work of all those who aim to preserve accurately Madiba's words and legacy is appreciated. Special thanks in relation to this project are due to Imani Media, Sarah Halfpenny, Richard Atkinson, and Brian Widlake.

For this edition we would like to thank Archbishop Desmond Tutu for his introduction. We would also like to extend our thanks to Lynn Franklin, and to Lara Love for her invaluable assistance in finalizing the selection of quotes you find here.

Select Bibliography

Books

Daymond, MJ, and Corinne Sandwith, eds. *Africa South: Viewpoints 1956–1961*. Scottsville, South Africa: University of KwaZulu-Natal Press, 2011.

Mandela, Nelson. *Conversations with Myself*. London: Macmillan Publishers, 2010; New York: Farrar, Straus and Giroux, 2010.

Mandela, Nelson. *Long Walk to Freedom*. London: Little, Brown and Company, 1994.

Meer, Fatima. *Higher Than Hope*. Johannesburg: Skotaville Publishers, 1988.

Nelson Mandela Foundation. *A Prisoner in the Garden: Opening Nelson Mandela's Prison Archive*. Johannesburg: Penguin, 2005.

Nicol, Mike. *Mandela: The Authorised Portrait*. Auckland, New Zealand: PQ Blackwell, 2006.

Villa-Vicencio, Charles. *The Spirit of Freedom: South African Leaders on Religion and Politics*. Berkeley and Los Angeles: University of California Press, 2006.

Documentaries

Countdown to Freedom: Ten Days that Changed South Africa, directed by Danny Schecter, Globalvision, USA, 1994.

The Last Mile: Mandela, Africa and Democracy, directed by Jennifer Pogrund, South Africa, 1992.

Legends: Nelson Mandela, directed by Walter Sucher, SWR, Germany, 2005.

Mandela at 90, directed by Clifford Bestall, Giant Media Productions, UK, 2008.

Mandela in America, directed by Danny Schechter, Globalvision, USA, 1990.

Mandela: Son of Africa, Father of a Nation, directed by Joe Menell and Angus Gibson, Clinica Estetico and Island Pictures, USA, 1996.

Mandela: The Living Legend, directed by Dominic Allan, BBC Television (UK), UK, 2003.

"Nelson Mandela," *Headliners and Legends*, MSNBC, USA, 2006.

Nelson Mandela Life Story, Imani Media for the Nelson Mandela Foundation, South Africa, 2008.

A South African Love Story: Walter and Albertina, directed by Toni Strasburg, XOXA Productions and Quest Star Communication, South Africa, 2004.

Viva Madiba: A Hero for All Seasons, directed by Catherine Meyburgh and Danny Schecter (consulting director), Videovision Entertainment, South Africa, 2010.

Website

www.nelsonmandela.org